ANIMAL TRACKS
of the Pacific Northwest

Text and Illustrations by
Karen Pandell and Chris Stall

THE MOUNTAINEERS • SEATTLE

The Mountaineers: Organized 1906 " . . . to explore, study,
preserve and enjoy the natural beauty of the Northwest."

Published by The Mountaineers,
306 2nd Ave. W., Seattle, Washington 98119

Published simultaneously in Canada
by Douglas & McIntyre, Ltd.
1615 Venables Street, Vancouver, British Columbia V5L 2H1

First edition: first printing March 1981, second printing October 1984,
third printing January 1987

Book design by Elizabeth Watson
Printed in the United States of America
Cover drawing: Badger tracks

Library of Congress Cataloging in Publication Data
Pandell, Karen.
  Animal Tracks of the Pacific Northwest.

  Includes index.
  1. Animal tracks — Northwest, Pacific. I. Stall,
Chris. II. Mountaineers (Society) III. Title.
QL768.P36   1981   599   81-2041
ISBN 0-89886-012-1   AACR2

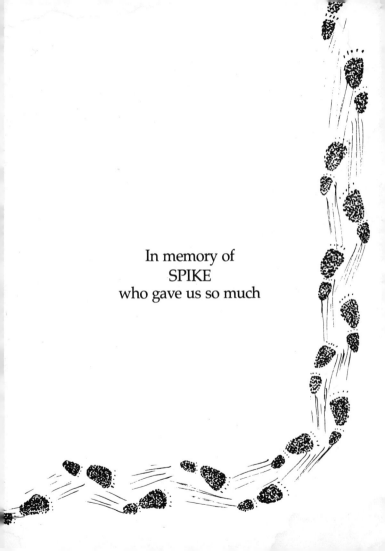

In memory of
SPIKE
who gave us so much

Contents

Introduction

Most wild animals in the Pacific Northwest, as in other areas, are either instinctively wary of humans or they have learned to be that way. Many animals must be shy and secretive in order to escape predators. Many are nocturnal and many fairly scarce. Most people don't have the time to make protracted journeys into the wildlands in order to catch glimpses of wild creatures.

Thus, tracks are the easy and obvious way to verify the presence of wild animals in any area. As with most things, once we found ourselves tuned in to tracks, we began to notice them everywhere. We finally became satisfied that lots of creatures were around after all, even though we couldn't see them.

We wanted to identify the animals making those tracks, and it appeared we had two alternatives. We could lug large field guides along with us or we could take paper and pencils to make field notes and sketches, which we could research after each trip. The latter method proved more practical, but we still had trouble waiting days to learn an item of information, not to mention trying to make sketches in mid-winter with the Alaska wind blowing at thirty miles per hour. We persevered, however, and after ten years of field work, we offer a third choice in the form of this compact book you are now holding.

You can use this book to identify an unknown track in the following manner:

1. Decide if the track was left by a bird or an animal — the two divisions of tracks in this book.
2. Note the size of the track. If each imprint is less than five inches long, you can hold the book right down next to the track itself and measure it, using the rule on the back cover.

3. Flip quickly through the appropriate section — bird or animal — until you find tracks that are roughly the same *size* as your mystery track. The tracks are organized roughly by size, from smallest in the front of the book to largest in the back.

4. Search carefully for the tracks in the book that, as closely as possible, match the *shape* of the unknown tracks.

5. If you can't find them, begin looking through the higher-numbered pages. You will no doubt find a larger version of the tracks you are looking for, at which time you'll know that yours were made by a young animal. Nearby you should be able to locate the tracks of its parent, which will more closely match the size of our drawing.

6. Finally, read the remarks, particularly on range, habitat, and track notes, to confirm the identification.

As you use this book, please bear the following in mind:

1. Track identification will be easier if you accept the premise that it is often an inexact science. Our drawings represent average adult tracks as we commonly found them on good surfaces. The wilds are full of smaller-than-average animals, particularly in late spring and early summer, also larger-than-average animals, injured or deformed animals, and animals that just don't act the way we think they should. Some are known to walk sideways on occasion. Most vary their gait so front tracks fall ahead for a while, then rear tracks appear ahead of front; then for another stretch the rear tracks exactly cover the front tracks. Animals often dislodge peripheral debris, which may further confuse the track picture; and ground conditions are usually less than ideal in the wild. Use this book as a guide, but anticipate lots of variations.

2. Overhanging trees, dripping on trails, often leave marks that could pass for the tracks of a mouse wearing shoepaks.

Try to be aware of similar non-animal factors that may leave "tracks."

3. The range listed concerns only the Pacific Northwest, which we think of as Oregon, Washington, British Columbia, and the Alaska panhandle. Most track makers in this book also live elsewhere in North America.

4. Both range and habitat notes are only general guidelines and are always subject to change with variations in animal populations, climatic factors, levels of pollution, human activities, volcanic eruptions, and so forth.

5. Size and weight are average guidelines for adult animals, with size being the length from nose to tip of tail. This is intended simply to give you a general mental image of the track maker if you are unfamiliar with the particular creature.

6. To keep our remarks brief and the book compact, we have made two assumptions: first, that you are already familiar with the general characteristics of the animal, and second, that you are willing to go to the nearest library or bookstore to do whatever supplemental research that might be required. A trip to a zoo that has indigenous wildlife on display can also be a worthwhile educational experience.

7. A few common species have been left out of this book: the mole, for instance, because it leaves no tracks as such; and the pika, because it lives below ground most of the summer and below snow most of the winter. Others in the book, particularly small rodents and birds, are included as representative of large groups of similar species. We have attempted to cover those that are most common and widely distributed.

8. You will find an occasional reference in this book to wild animals that have been kept as pets. When you encounter an injured or orphaned animal, there is often a great temptation to take it home and care for it. In addition to the rules

of common sense, U.S. and Canadian regulations often strictly control the handling of wild animals. Be sure to check with local authorities to determine whether adoption is legal.

9. Finally, this book is largely a compilation of our own personal experiences. Your experiences with certain animals and their tracks may be identical, similar, or even quite different from ours. Don't be confused if you notice a discrepancy. You might even encounter tracks of an animal that we have not included. You can use the blank pages at the back of the book for field notes detailing your own observations, or amend the illustrations or text to reflect your experiences. This book was designed to be *used* as a field tool in forming a general foundation for the practice of identifying animal tracks in the Pacific Northwest.

Animal tracks may be something you concern yourself with only when you stumble upon them. On the other hand, locating and identifying tracks can become obsessive. You find yourself walking around with your chin resting securely on your breastbone, staring feverishly at the ground. You find yourself eagerly anticipating the snow season, because tracks are so much more plentiful then. Just about every creature that is out and about in winter leaves tracks in snow, so that winter excursions become gourmet delights for track-consuming hikers.

In the absence of snow, you may work harder to adjust your routes, avoiding bedrock and ground cover, and seeking out damp sand or soft dirt in river courses, near ponds, bogs, lakes, or at the ocean. You might venture into the desert in early morning, before the sand becomes dry and disturbed by the wind. After rainfall, you might go out looking for patches of virgin mud, especially along dirt roads and hiking trails, where even among remnant tread marks and hiking boot imprints the animal tracks are always fresh and clear.

Whatever your degree of interest, in backyard or deep wilderness, we hope you will enjoy using this book to identify animal tracks for as long as you need it, and that your interest continues until you reach a level of proficiency at which this book is no longer needed.

ANIMALS

DEER MOUSE
White-footed mouse

Peromyscus maniculatus

Order: Rodentia. Family: Cricetidae (New World rats and mice). Range: common throughout the Pacific Northwest. Habitat: all areas at all altitudes; most common in woodlands and adjoining areas, occasionally around abandoned buildings; prefers country to inhabited areas. Size and weight: seven inches; one ounce. Diet: omnivorous, including seeds, plant greens, mushrooms, insects, grubs, caterpillars, carrion. Sounds: faint bird-like trills and chattering squeaks.

The native, wide-ranging and common deer mouse, with its long tail and pretty white undersides and feet, is primarily a mouse of the wilds, although it may nest in old buildings in the country and occasionally ventures into occupied dwellings. Active year-around, the deer mouse is a good climber and runner and is generally nocturnal. These tiny creatures make up the main diets of many carnivorous birds and mammals, but they are not totally defenseless. They can bite, as anyone who has tried to handle an injured mouse without gloves will tell you.

The deer mouse hardly ever moves slowly. It usually leaves a distinctive leaping four-print pattern, with the tail dragging only occasionally. The mouse is so small and light that its tracks are distinct only on rare occasions when surface conditions are perfect. More often you may find a line composed of groups of four tiny dimples in a mud or snow surface. The tracks could also be made by the ubiquitous house mouse (if in the vicinity of inhabited dwellings) or by the little pocket mouse, great basin pocket mouse, harvest mouse, canyon mouse, piñon mouse, and many others. Give or take an inch in length and a few ounces in weight, all Pacific Northwest mice are quite similar in appearance. A good pictorial field guide and some patient field work will be required for positive identification of each. Generally, mouse tracks can be distinguished from shrew tracks because the track clusters are wider than the shrew's and because the mouse's tail drag marks are either erratic or absent while the shrew's are prominent.

Deer Mouse
life size in mud

DUSKY SHREW

Sorex obscurus

Order: Insectivora. Family: Soricidae (shrews). Range: southeastern Alaska through northern Washington. Habitat: moist areas in forests and meadows. Size and weight: five inches; one ounce. Diet: insects, small animals, carrion. Sounds: generally silent; occasional diminutive squeaks.

The dusky shrew, the most wide-ranging Pacific Northwest shrew, lives a life of gluttony. Due to the high rate of shrew metabolism, it must eat every twenty-four hours an amount of food equivalent to its own body weight. It eats around the clock summer and winter alike, usually every two to three hours.

Other Pacific Northwest shrews include the masked shrew, found in most of non-desert Washington, British Columbia, and southeastern Alaska; the Merriam shrew of eastern Washington and Oregon; and the Malheur shrew, found in desert areas of Washington and Oregon. All are very similar in proportion to the dusky shrew, and field sightings will help you identify locally prevalent species.

Primarily because shrews are so light in weight, it is unusual to find shrew tracks unless the animals have been scurrying over fresh, fine mud or snow. Their tiny tracks are seen everywhere after a snowfall. Shrew tracks might be confused with those of various mice, but close inspection will reveal shrew trails to be at least half an inch narrower than most mice trails. Also, shrew tracks generally have an etched unbroken line between the pairs of miniscule footprints, caused by the dragging tail.

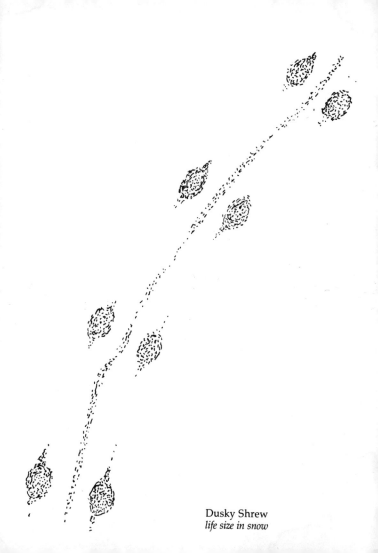

Dusky Shrew
life size in snow

YELLOW-PINE CHIPMUNK   *Eutamias amoenus*

Order: Rodentia. Family: Sciuridae (squirrels). Range: British Columbia through Oregon. Habitat: open pine forests; rocky, brushy areas; and chaparral, at various altitudes. Size and weight: eight inches; four ounces. Diet: insects, plants, seeds, and grain. Sounds: a shrill "chip, chip, chip."

Named for its principal habitat, the yellow-pine chipmunk is a comical little animal that scampers along logs with its tail pointed straight up. It is primarily an animal of the forest floor, where it seeks out burrows and conducts most of its activities, but it does occasionally climb trees. It transports seeds and other food items in cheek pouches, looking like an animal with mumps. Chipmunks are frequently encountered at picnic spots and campgrounds, where they readily accept a variety of junk food, not stopping to eat, but carting the assorted items off to cache sites as fast as they can run.

Other Pacific Northwest chipmunks, quite similar in appearance and difficult to distinguish in the field, include the Townsend chipmunk of eastern Washington, Oregon, and portions of southeastern British Columbia; the least chipmunk, in parts of central and eastern Washington and Oregon; and the redtail chipmunk, in eastern Washington and southeastern British Columbia.

The track patterns of the chipmunk are 1⅞ to 2½ inches in width, with seven to fifteen inches between groups of prints. Chipmunks often run up on their toes, and the heel imprints will not show. The hind foot tracks always fall in front of the forefoot tracks, as is true of all squirrels. If these tracks are found in mid-winter, you can assume they were formed by a smallish squirrel, rather than a chipmunk, since chipmunks tend to hole up with their stored food treasures in mid-winter. At all other times of the year, the fact that squirrels spend most of their time in trees should help you determine the track origin.

Yellow-Pine Chipmunk
life size in mud

MEADOW VOLE
Meadow mouse, field mouse

Microtus pennsylvanicus

Order: Rodentia. Family: Cricetidae (New World rats and mice). Range: southeastern Alaska through northern Washington. Habitat: moist areas in forests and meadows. Size and weight: six inches; four ounces. Diet: grain, grasses, bulbs, bark, flowers, seeds. Sounds: generally quiet; occasional small squeaks.

On a camping trip, we awoke one morning to see a meadow vole stealthily making trips back and forth from our food cache. Closer inspection at the scene of the "crime" showed that the vole had gnawed a hole in our bag of granola. Bit by bit it was spiriting away the contents of the bag.

The meadow vole is a plump and sprightly little ball of dark gray or brown fur. It goes about its activities year-around, eating by day and night. Do not be surprised if you see a tiny vole moving around in the water. They are expert swimmers and use their aquatic skills to cross streams and travel in marshy areas.

Many other species of voles and vole-like animals live in portions of the Pacific Northwest, including the widespread longtail vole, the sagebrush, Richardson, Oregon, Townsend, mountain, and tundra voles, as well as several species of redback voles, lemmings, and phenacomys. All are nearly indistinguishable from the meadow vole in appearance, habits, and tracks. Careful field observations would be required to determine the exact identity of specific track makers in your locale.

Vole tracks in mud show the four toes on the front paw and the five toes on the back. The distance between track clusters changes with speed, but generally averages two to three inches. Voles are inclined to a ground-hugging mode of travel. Mice, on the other hand, generally travel in leaps, averaging five to six inches between track groups.

Meadow Vole
life size in dust

BOREAL TOAD
Western toad

Bufo boreas

Order: Salientia. Family: Bufonidae (true toads). Range: southeastern Alaska through Oregon. Habitat: coastal forests and adjoining areas. Size and weight: three inches; two ounces. Diet: insects. Sounds: generally silent.

We first became aware of the abundance of boreal toads in the Pacific Northwest by observing them at our building site near Glacier Bay, Alaska. We dug deep holes for our foundation posts and each morning had to rescue several hapless toads that had fallen into the holes during the night. For a time we nicknamed our building site "Toad Hall" in honor of them.

Unlike frogs, boreal toads often travel far from bodies of water. They may be brown, green, or gray with skin that is dry and warty in appearance. Their bodies are squat and chunky. These delightful Buddha-like creatures consume prodigious amounts of insects. If you wish to hold a toad, be sure your hands are free of insect repellent, which can cause severe skin damage to these animals.

When you find toad tracks, you will see wispy scuffling marks. Toads would rather walk than hop. Note also the pigeon-toed gait.

Boreal Toad
life size in mud

SPOTTED FROG

Rana pretiosa

Order: Salientia. Family: Ranidae (true frogs). Range: southeastern Alaska through Oregon. Habitat: coastal forests and marshy areas near year-around bodies of water. Size and weight: three inches; two ounces. Diet: insects. Sounds: low-pitched croaks.

The spotted frog is smooth-skinned and streamlined as a bullet. It has spots on its back and salmon-pink undersides.

The Latin name *Rana* for the genus of this frog is derived from a Sanskrit root, meaning "one who utters a sound." The spotted frog has a low, rich voice, which it uses above and below water. The species name is *pretiosa* or "precious." This active, glistening amphibian eats enormous amounts of insects during its lifetime, which makes it especially "precious" to those who hike in the woodlands. As with the boreal toad, be sure your hands are free of insect repellent when handling this animal.

Spotted frogs have long muscular legs and excel in jumping, as their tracks show. The tracks might be confused with the toad's, but toads usually walk rather than hop. Frog tracks will be found near water; you won't find them along hiking trails or in other woodland places far from bodies of water, as you might the toad's.

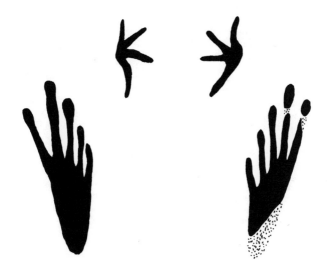

Spotted Frog
life size in mud

SHORT-TAIL WEASEL
Ermine

Mustela ermina

Order: Carnivora. Family: Mustelidae (weasels). Range: southeastern Alaska through Oregon. Habitat: varied, from lowland forests to mountain talus slopes. Size and weight: twelve inches; eight ounces. Diet: rodents, including mice, chipmunks, ground squirrels, and moles. Sounds: generally silent; may squeal occasionally.

One morning we took Spike, our pet porcupine, for a stroll near our cottage at Glacier Bay, Alaska. Out from under our lumber pile darted a slender, brown animal with a pencil-thin tail. We held still as it peered at Spike intently for a few seconds. It evidently decided that our porcupine was a bit too big to take on, as it would come no closer. This inquisitive, feisty animal was the short-tail weasel. Since this was during the early fall, our nosy neighbor had a dark brown coat with white underneath. In winter, it has a white coat.

Weasels have five toes on each foot, but the fifth may not show in the track imprint. The track pattern shows two prints side by side forming a line of double tracks. The weasel's hind tracks usually cover the front tracks as it travels energetically through its hunting grounds. Scanning a weasel's trail, one can't help but admire the tracks as calligraphy. The animal darts in all sorts of loops, curlicues, and turns in its constant search for food.

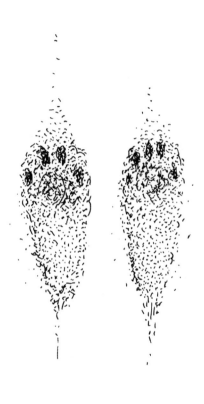

Short-Tail Weasel
life size in snow

CHICKAREE
Douglas squirrel
RED SQUIRREL

Tamiasciurus douglasi

Tamiasciurus hudsonicus

Order: Rodentia. Family: Sciuridae (squirrels). Range: chickaree: southern British Columbia through Oregon; red squirrel: southeastern Alaska to British Columbia, northeastern areas of Washington and Oregon. Habitat: coniferous forests. Size and weight: twelve inches; nine ounces. Diet: pine and spruce cone seeds, willow catkin seeds, fruits, nuts, fungi, insects, buds, and flowers. Sounds: scolds, chatters, churrs.

Chickarees and red squirrels have the same habits and track patterns. The difference between them lies in the color of their coats. The chickaree is dusky-olive above and buff-yellow below. The red squirrel has a reddish-gray coat above and white underneath. These squirrels are active all day and at all times of the year. They are especially busy during the early fall. One September on a walk through the woods, we heard mysterious thumping sounds. We happened to look to the top of an eighty-foot spruce tree where a red squirrel was energetically heaving cones to the ground like a gnome-sized dock-worker unloading freight. It pitched cones for a while, then scampered down the trunk to gather them for its winter food cache.

Squirrel tracks have definite toenail imprints, because squirrels have curved toenails that act as hooks for tree climbing. The track shows the squirrel's four toes on its front foot and five toes on its hind foot. Oftentimes the heel mark will not show. Spacing between the tracks may vary widely as squirrels leap from eight to thirty inches.

Also present in the Coast Range forests of Washington and Oregon is the western gray squirrel. This animal, somewhat larger than the other Pacific Northwest tree squirrels, is gray with white undersides and has a long, bushy tail. Its habits are very similar to the two mentioned above, as are its tracks, except that they are somewhat larger. Gray squirrel track clusters will be up to 4¾ inches in width, and up to thirty-six inches apart when the animals are running.

Chickaree and Red Squirrel
life size in mud

COLUMBIAN GROUND SQUIRREL   *Citellus columbianus*

Order: Rodentia. Family: Sciuridae (squirrels). Range: southeastern British Columbia through eastern Washington and Oregon. Habitat: plains, meadows, grasslands, dry and sandy soils in or adjoining areas of green vegetation (including farmland), and desert areas. Size and weight: fifteen inches; ¾ to 1½ pounds. Diet: omnivorous, including green vegetation, some grains, seeds, fruits, birds, bird eggs, insects, and carrion, including its own species. Sounds: brief and abrupt high-pitched chirps and whistles.

The Columbian ground squirrel is the largest of the numerous species of ground squirrel in the Pacific Northwest, including the California of western Oregon; Belding, Townsend, and Washington of eastern Oregon; Arctic of northcentral British Columbia; and the golden-mantled of Oregon and the Cascades, which looks somewhat like a large chipmunk. Field observations and note taking, assisted by a good pictorial field guide, will help you determine which species inhabits your particular area.

All species are colonial animals, denning in burrows or occasionally beneath rocks, logs, and stumps, where they store food. They have several den entrances, each about three inches in diameter. In the Pacific Northwest, ground squirrels are generally gray with various subtle coat patterns.

The track shape and print pattern are similar for all ground squirrels. The truncated inner toe on the front foot often leaves a slight imprint on soft surfaces. Generally eight to sixteen inches separate groups of four prints made by running animals; they usually walk only at den entrances where you may find the spacing between individual prints totally random. Ground squirrels seem to be more flat-footed than tree squirrels. Also, tree squirrel tracks always lead to, and are never far from, trees. Conversely, ground squirrel tracks never go far from, and always lead back to, their burrows. Also, ground squirrel claws are fairly straight and usually don't leave marks, whereas tree squirrels have curved claws, adapted to vertical climbing and clinging to bark, which tend to leave tiny marks. Finally, tree squirrels are active all winter; while ground squirrel tracks may be encountered in early fall or late spring snow, they will be absent for the winter.

Columbian Ground Squirrel
life size in sand

NORTHERN FLYING SQUIRREL   *Glaucomys sabrinus*

Order: Rodentia. Family: Sciuridae (squirrels). Range: southeastern Alaska through Oregon. Habitat: coniferous forests. Size and weight: ten inches; three ounces. Diet: bark, fungi, lichen, insects, birds' eggs. Sounds: generally silent; makes a "click" sound when landing on a tree.

Many people in the Pacific Northwest are unaware of the northern flying squirrel's presence. These aerial creatures sleep all day and go about their activities at night. A silky-gray, fur-covered membrane extends between the animal's front and hind paws. Add to this its flattened tail, which acts like a rudder, and you have a square-shaped creature well-adapted for hang-gliding from tree to tree or tree to ground.

During most of the year, you will seldom find any evidence of this animal's tracks since it leaves no prints in the soft needles of the pine and spruce forest floor. In snow the scampering squirrel track pattern is more easily seen. Places where a flying squirrel has landed in the snow look like miniature snow angel patterns.

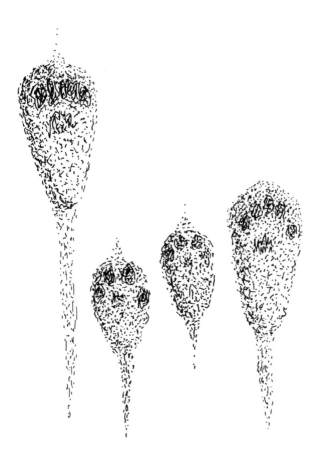

Northern Flying Squirrel
life size in snow

BUSHY-TAILED WOOD RAT
Cave rat, pack rat

Neotoma cinerea

Order: Rodentia. Family: Cricetidae (New World rats and mice). Range: throughout the Pacific Northwest except offshore islands. Habitat: cliffs, caves, rock and talus areas at all elevations; also abandoned buildings. Size and weight: fourteen inches; eight ounces. Diet: largely vegetarian; occasionally larvae, insects, and carrion. Sounds: non-vocal, but may drum and thump with feet and tail when alarmed.

This native American rat is generally nocturnal, active in all seasons, and eats nearly everything. Not to be confused with the Norway rat and other ugly imports, our bushy-tailed wood rat avoids humans and inhabited areas, although it may "borrow" shiny and otherwise attractive objects from campsites in its territory.

Bushy-tailed wood rats have fairly stubby toes that leave unique tracks. Running, they leave groups of four prints about every eight inches. Like most small rodents, when the wood rat leaps, its front feet land first, then the back feet come down together ahead of the front feet and provide the spring into the next leap. Thus, the illustrated tracks show the back prints ahead of the front prints.

Two other wood rats are present in the Pacific Northwest — the desert wood rat, found on the desert floor of southeastern Oregon, and the dusky-footed wood rat, living in wooded parts of western Oregon. Both species are slightly smaller than the bushy-tailed and lack bushy hair on their tails, but their feet have the same stubby toes. Their tracks are quite similar to those illustrated, if very slightly smaller.

Bushy-Tailed Wood Rat
life size in mud

MINK

Mustela vison

Order: Carnivora. Family: Mustelidae (weasels). Range: southeastern Alaska through Oregon. Habitat: woodland areas near streams, lakes, and other bodies of water. Size and weight: two feet; three pounds. Diet: fish, frogs, salamanders, snakes, water birds, eggs, and all smaller mammals. Sounds: squeals, hisses.

The dark brown mink is as sleek as any weasel and as exuberantly playful as a river otter. It finds its food by fishing for turtles, fish, and crayfish in fresh-water streams and lakes or prospecting for morsels in seashore tidepools. This generally nocturnal animal is active year-around, with dens in stream or river banks, hollow logs, rock or brush piles, or abandoned muskrat nests. At the seashore, it may have a beach house in a pile of driftwood.

Mink tracks give a clue to the nature of this frenetic little hunter that darts in all directions and investigates every nook and cranny in its near-constant search for food. Between a weasel and marten in size, the spacing between groups of four tracks or the more characteristic double pair of tracks is usually about twenty inches. Mink tracks are also readily identified because they are almost always found near water.

Mink
life size in mud

MOUNTAIN BEAVER
Aplodontia

Aplodontia rufa

Order: Rodentia. Family: Aplodontiidae. Range: southwestern British Columbia through Oregon. Habitat: most coastal rainforests. Size and weight: thirteen inches; three pounds. Diet: berry bushes, bracken fern, skunk cabbage, nettles, devil's club. Sounds: generally silent; occasionally whistles, grunts; softly whimpers and cries if injured.

People in the Pacific Northwest have a remarkable animal in their midst — the mountain beaver or aplodontia. It is the oldest living rodent species and makes its home only in the Pacific Northwest. This appealing brown rodent has a blunt snout, small black myopic eyes, and almost no tail at all. Basically a quiet and shy creature, it pursues its interests in areas of dense vegetation. When hiking on coastal trails, you may come upon evidence of its burrows or haymaking. It devotes springtime to excavating extensive burrow systems in moist earth near flowing water. In late summer it begins to pile plants on logs to dry for winter use. The mountain beaver should be applauded by all back country hikers as it eats, among other things, nettles and devil's club.

The mountain beaver track is not apt to be confused with that of any other animal. The track imprint in mud shows its distinctively long and slender toes. It is a small, slow-moving animal, consequently leaving a trail of closely spaced tracks.

Mountain Beaver
life size in mud

MUSKRAT   *Ondatra zibethica*

Order: Rodentia. Family: Cricetidae (New World rats and mice). Range: widespread and common throughout the Pacific Northwest. Habitat: fresh-water marshes, streams, lakes, and ponds. Size and weight: two feet; three pounds. Diet: omnivorous including aquatic plants and small aquatic animals such as snails, tadpoles, and shellfish, particularly fresh-water mussels. Sounds: high-pitched squeaks.

The muskrat is a large rat modified for an aquatic life by the addition of a flattened, scaly, rudder-like tail and partially webbed hind feet. Like the beaver, it has been a commercially important fur bearer for several centuries. Muskrats associate readily with beavers and occasionally nest within the confines of beaver lodges. Most of the time they burrow into river banks or construct lodges similar to the beavers', but smaller and made of lighter materials, primarily grasses. They are basically nocturnal, but can be seen occasionally during the day or at dusk, parting the still surface of the water, tail skulling along, mouth full of grass for its nest.

Muskrat tracks are nearly always found in mud close to water. It is one of the few rodents with five toes on its front feet although the small inner toe often fails to leave a mark. At the water's edge, the muskrat leaves tracks two to three inches apart when walking, twelve inches when running. The hind foot tracks are most distinctive, with the tail sometimes dragging. The hind feet have a stiff webbing of hair between the toes.

Muskrat
life size in mud

OPOSSUM

Didelphis marsupialis

Order: Marsupialia (pouched mammals). Family: Didelphiidae. Range: central and western Washington and Oregon. Habitat: woodlands and adjoining areas, generally remaining near streams and lakes; farming areas. Size and weight: twenty-five inches; fifteen pounds. Diet: an opportunistic omnivore, prefers fruits, vegetables, insects, small mammals, birds, eggs, carrion, also garbage and pet food. Sounds: generally silent; a gurgling hiss when annoyed.

On one hand, the opossum appears quite ordinary: it looks like a large, long-haired rat, with pointed nose, light gray and white fur, and a long, scaly, reptilian tail. It is largely terrestrial, finds burrows in the ground, but will climb to escape danger. The opossum is generally nocturnal and other than climbing, its only defense mechanism is an ability to feign death, or "play possum."

Yet in many respects, the opossum is easily the most peculiar animal residing on this continent. Among the oldest and most primitive of all living mammals, it has the only prehensile (used for grasping) tail in North America. It is the only non-primate in the animal kingdom with an opposable digit, the inside toes on the hind feet. And it is the only marsupial (pouched animal) on our continent. As many as twenty young are born prematurely, after only thirteen days of gestation, weighing 1/15 ounce each (the whole litter would fit into a teaspoon!). The tiny young crawl into their mother's pouch, where they remain for the next two months, often riding around on the mother's back for some time after they emerge from the pouch.

Happily, these curious animals leave easily identifiable tracks. Those opposable hind thumbs create unique prints, sometimes pointing as much as ninety degrees or more from the direction of travel. Like raccoons, opossums leave tracks in a row of pairs, each group of two consisting of one front and one rear foot imprint, always close to, or slightly overlapping, each other. The distance between pairs will be from five to eleven inches, depending on the animal's size and speed of travel. The opossum's long tail frequently leaves drag marks in snow or mud.

Opossum
life size in mud

HOARY MARMOT

Marmota caligata

Order: Rodentia. Family: Sciuridae (squirrels). Range: widespread throughout southeastern Alaska and British Columbia; in the Cascades of central Washington. Habitat: high mountain talus slopes and boulder fields, often in rocks amid forests at high altitudes. Size and weight: 2½ feet; fifteen pounds. Diet: strictly herbivorous, including foliage and succculent alpine grasses and flowers. Sounds: a high, plaintive, drawn-out whistle.

The largest American squirrel, the hoary marmot sleeps more than any other mammal on the continent, hibernating from October through April, and sleeping at night during its short summer. It is covered with light gray fur and has black feet and black and white face markings. Fairly easy to find in the wild, it gives its location away with its piercing whistle, employed as both an alarm and as a means of keeping tabs on its fellow marmots' locations. A marmot's favorite daytime activities are eating and sunbathing on a prominent lookout rock. Its eyesight is not particularly good. If you stay downwind and move slowly, you should have no trouble sneaking in for a closer look.

The hoary marmot's tracks are identical to those of its cousin, the yellow-bellied marmot of eastern Oregon and Washington. The four front toes and five rear ones are typically rodent; the heel pads of the front feet are distinctive. The ranges of the two marmots do not overlap, but in the event that you've lost track of your location, the short, chopped-off call of the yellow-bellied marmot may help with identification in the absence of field sightings.

Hoary Marmot
life size in mud

MARTEN
Pine marten, sable

Martes americana

Order: Carnivora. Family: Mustelidae (weasels). Range: throughout the Pacific Northwest. Habitat: coniferous forests and adjoining areas, occasionally rock slide areas. Size and weight: two feet; five pounds. Diet: generally carnivorous, including mice, rats, squirrels, and small birds and eggs; berries and nuts. Sounds: generally silent.

Between a mink and fisher in size, the marten is typically weasel in appearance, with buffy fur on its throat and light yellow-brown fur overall. It is an adaptable, energetic, solitary animal that is usually nocturnal and always extremely wary, and thus is sighted infrequently in the wild. Marten cover distances of many miles in a single night's hunting. They are active all year, denning in tree cavities or on the ground. They are great tree climbers and are largely arboreal, not the least oriented toward aquatic environs, although they are found in areas where dense coniferous forest extends right to the ocean's edge.

Marten leave few signs other than tracks, and these are scarce before snow falls. Then, their tracks tend to lead to and from trees and rarely venture near water as the mink's usually do. Small, thin pads behind five toes and nails are normally visible in marten tracks, with size and spacing definitely larger than mink. Walking tracks are six to nine inches apart; running, two feet separating groups of four prints; leaping, pairs of overlapping prints four feet apart.

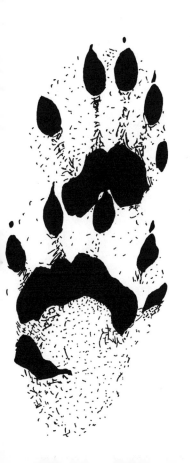

Marten
life size in mud

STRIPED SKUNK   *Mephitis mephitis*

Order: Carnivora. Family: Mustelidae (weasels). Range: southern half of British Columbia through Oregon. Habitat: all land areas. Size and weight: thirty inches; ten pounds. Diet: insects, field mice, fish, crayfish. Sounds: twitters, scolds, chatters.

The striped skunk packs away enormous quantities of food during the spring, summer, and fall. It would undoubtedly be an extremely obese little animal if it did not go on a crash diet every winter. It does not hibernate or cache extra food for the winter; and due to the scarcity of winter food, the skunk's weight often drops to half that of its summer bulk.

Although few animals are foolish enough to tangle with a skunk, it is actually quite an amiable creature, preferring to be left alone to wander about in search of delicious morsels. It stamps its feet to give those who annoy it fair warning. If the threatening animal does not leave immediately, the skunk lets go its spray, an oily yellow liquid that can cause temporary blindness for up to twenty minutes.

Another unique skunk activity has been reported by many observers. Skunks sometimes hold group dances in the moonlight. Two lines of skunks form a circle. Holding their tails high, they all dance in unison to the center of the circle until their noses touch, then move back to make the circle again. These rhythmic movements are repeated as many as ten times.

The striped skunk has non-retractable claws, which leave clear imprints in almost any surface. The skunk walks flat-footed, and its five-inch stride reflects the purposeful travel of a calm, shuffling, portly animal. The skunk's spray weaponry replaces any requirement for speed.

Striped Skunk
life size in mud

BOBCAT
Wildcat, bay lynx

Lynx rufus

Order: Carnivora. Family: Felidae (cats). Range: throughout Oregon and Washington; rare in southern British Columbia. Habitat: equally at home in swamp, rainforest, desert, forested mountainous terrain. Size and weight: three feet; thirty pounds. Diet: strictly carnivorous, including birds, small mammals, and young deer. Sounds: typical domestic cat sounds with slightly more volume.

Closely related to the lynx, the bobcat is a very adaptable animal that is afield both day and night, and occasionally wanders into suburban areas. It is a ground hunter, but will climb trees and drop onto unexpecting prey. You might mistake it for a large tabby cat with a bobbed tail, but there the similarity ends, for bobcats have quite wild dispositions, combined with much greater strength and razor-sharp claws and teeth.

You can expect to encounter bobcat tracks almost anywhere. You will know they are cat tracks because the four retractile claws on each foot never leave imprints, and the toes usually spread a bit more than a dog's. Bobcat tracks are too large to confuse with those of a domestic cat, and are clearly smaller than those of lynx or cougar. Also, domestic cats have pads that are single-lobed at the front end.

Bobcat
life size in mud

RED FOX

Vulpes fulva

Order: Carnivora. Family: Canidae (dogs). Range: throughout the Pacific Northwest except the Olympic Peninsula or arid regions of eastern Washington and Oregon. Habitat: woodlands and adjoining areas, especially mountainous areas near timberline. Size and weight: forty-four inches; eight pounds. Diet: small mammals including marmots, chipmunks, squirrels, and hares; also fruits, berries, grains, grasses, birds, reptiles, and amphibians. Sounds: a variety of noises from barks to screams.

The intelligence of the fox has been celebrated in literature since Aesop recorded his fables in 500 B.C. The fox often finds food easily by following the trail of an animal, such as a wolverine, that has made a food cache. An adult fox does not sleep in a den in the winter. It curls its comely tail around its nose to form a warm furry package. The fox may become covered by snow during a storm; perhaps some of the small, snowy hummocks you see in winter are actually sleeping foxes.

The front track of the fox is wide while the rear track is narrower. In some prints in snow, only a partial pad will show, making the heel and toe marks clearly separate. Red fox tracks could be mistaken for domestic dog tracks but for its eighteen-inch stride, somewhat longer than that of a similar-sized dog. A special feature to look for in identifying red fox tracks is the curved bar on the heel pad.

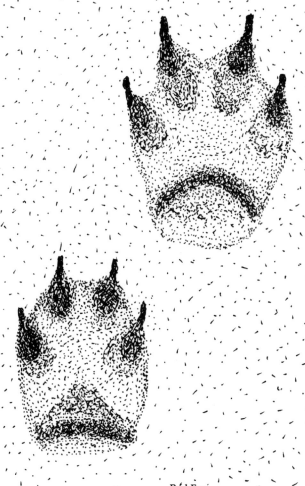

Red Fox
life size in sand

BADGER

Taxidea taxus

Order: Carnivora. Family: Mustelidae (weasels). Range: southern British Columbia through central and eastern Washington and Oregon. Habitat: treeless meadow and semi-open prairie at all altitudes, wherever ground-dwelling rodents are abundant. Size and weight: 2½ feet; twenty pounds. Diet: strictly carnivorous, including all smaller rodents; also snakes, birds, eggs, insects, and carrion. Sounds: may snarl or hiss when alarmed.

The badger is a solitary creature that digs up most of its food and tunnels into the earth to escape danger. Its powerful short legs and long strong claws are nicely suited for its earthmoving lifestyle. Above ground, the badger is a fierce fighter, threatened by only the larger carnivores. Its facial markings are quite distinctive and easily recognized: light brown or gray coarse body fur and a black face with white ears and cheeks and a white stripe running from its nose over the top of its head. The animal goes out in daylight and is not too shy, even entering campgrounds in its search for small rodents, its dietary staple.

Badger tracks show five long, clear toe prints of each foot and obvious marks left by the long front claws. The animal walks on its soles, which may or may not leave complete prints. Its pigeon-toed trail may be confused with the porcupine's in deep snow, but the porcupine trail will invariably lead to a tree or into a natural den, while the badger's leads to a burrow of its own making. Too, the badger's soft tail rarely leaves marks.

Badger
life size in mud

COYOTE
Brush wolf, prairie wolf

Canis latrans

Order: Carnivora. Family: Canidae (dogs). Range: throughout the Pacific Northwest except offshore islands. Habitat: desert, plains, forests at all altitudes; prefers open areas; extremely adaptable. Size and weight: four feet; forty pounds. Diet: Omnivorous, including fruit and berries, insects, fish, birds, mice, ground squirrels, other small mammals, and carrion. Sounds: barks, growls; packs yelp in high-pitched chorus.

Coyotes — important controllers of small rodents — are expanding their range. They are very smart, adaptable animals, good runners and swimmers, and have great stamina. Still, they are shy and generally not seen often in the wild.

Typically canine, the coyote's front paw is slightly larger than the rear, and the front toes tend to spread wider, though not as wide as the bobcat's. Toenails nearly always leave imprints, and the shape of coyote pads is unique, the front differing markedly from the rear. This characteristic, plus the lengthy stride (sixteen inches walking and leaps to ten feet) may help you distinguish their tracks from those of foxes or domestic dogs. Also, coyotes carry their tails down, leaving imprints in deep snow.

Coyote
life size in mud

FISHER
Black cat

Martes pennanti

Order: Carnivora. Family: Mustelidae (weasels). Range: central and western Oregon and Washington up through southern half of British Columbia. Habitat: primarily coniferous forest, usually at lower elevations. Size and weight: three feet; twelve pounds. Diet: strictly carnivorous, including insects, frogs, fish, birds, eggs, and all smaller mammals including weasels and porcupines. Sounds: hisses, growls, and snarls.

Fishers like fish when they find them washed up, but will not enter water to catch them. Between a marten and wolverine in size, they are easily identified by their weasel family appearance: dark fur and a foot-long, bushy, tapering tail. Fishers are very aggressive animals, strong for their size, fast-moving on the ground, and one of the world's fastest tree-climbing mammals. Consequently, their diets often consist of weasel family cousins.

Because fishers are fairly scarce, nocturnal, and prefer deep coniferous forests, they are seldom seen in the wild. But they are active year-around, and their tracks are easy enough to recognize. Typical of the weasel clan, all five toes and claws usually leave marks, as do the rather narrow pads. Fisher tracks will generally lead to or away from trees and will avoid water. Walking prints are ten to fifteen inches apart while running tracks are three to four feet apart, and leaping pairs of overlapping prints are four to six feet apart.

Fisher
life size in mud

PORCUPINE
Porky, quill pig

Erethizon dorsatum

Order: Rodentia. Family: Erethizontidae. Range: common throughout most of the Pacific Northwest except offshore islands. Habitat: forests, fields, semi-desert; a very adaptable animal. Size and weight: three feet; twenty-five pounds average, some reach forty pounds. Diet: strictly vegetarian, including succulents, willow leaves, bark, fruits, nuts, and many wild flowers. Sounds: generally quiet, but capable of a great variety of grunts, whines, and many harmonica-like noises; also clicks teeth together rapidly.

Porcupines are one of the few animals whose tracks you can follow with reasonable expectation of sighting their maker, because they move quite slowly when not alarmed, are often out during daylight hours, and do not see well. So if you stay downwind and quiet, you can usually observe these peaceable animals at your leisure. An alarmed porcupine climbs a tree to escape danger and uses its quills only as a last-ditch defense against an outright attack.

Porcupines may be slow-moving, but they are actually quite intelligent. We rescued an injured, week-old porcupine from the middle of a road once. It had problems with its feet and could not be expected to survive in the wilderness. So it lived in our house for two years, proving to be a wonderful pet. It had a wide range of emotions, loved to be handled, and never bored our guests.

Often the distinctive shuffling gait and dragging whisk-broom tail may be the only clear track signs, especially in deep snow. In winter the porcupine trail generally leads to and ends at a large coniferous tree. Once in a while a flat piece of snow or mud that has adhered to the porcupine's foot will be dislodged intact, revealing the unique pebbled texture of its sole. Imprints from the long claws may also be present.

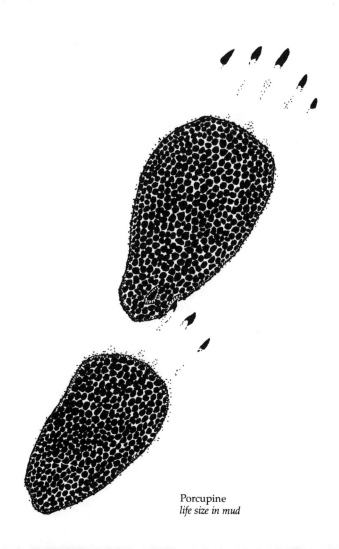

Porcupine
life size in mud

RACCOON

Procyon lotor

Order: Carnivora. Family: Procyonidae. Range: southern British Columbia through Oregon. Habitat: near streams and lakes. Size and weight: 2½ feet; thirty-five pounds. Diet: crayfish, fish, frogs, mice, larger insects, birds and their eggs, berries, fruits, vegetables. Sounds: a wide variety of noises including shrill cries, whistles, churrs, growls, screams.

The raccoon combines its curiosity with the manual dexterity of a surgeon. We have heard stories about a pet raccoon in Oregon that liked to gently touch people's faces with its hands. Its favorite trick was to pull pants pockets inside-out on washing day. Raccoons have also been observed performing self-surgery with their teeth on feet injured by a bullet or trap; after the "operation," they clean the wounds in running water.

The *"lotor"* in *Procyon lotor* means "one who washes." Since raccoons like to wash their food, you can often find their tracks near water. The tracks of the raccoon in mud look remarkably like those of a human baby's hand. Both front and back feet have five toes. When the raccoon walks, the left back foot track is placed next to the right front foot track and so forth to form paired tracks. When running, all four tracks tend to bunch together. The stride of the raccoon is about seven inches with leaps of twenty inches.

Raccoon
life size in mud

RIVER OTTER
Land otter

Lutra canadensis

Order: Carnivora. Family: Mustelidae (weasels). Range: southeastern Alaska through Oregon. Habitat: in or near lakes, streams, and coastal ocean areas. Size and weight: forty-eight inches; twenty pounds. Diet: fish, turtles, frogs, crayfish, snakes, birds and their eggs. Sounds: chirps, chatters, chuckles, grunts.

On a sub-zero day in January we had the pleasure of observing a river otter at close range near the inlet of a frozen lake. Even out of water it retained its fluid gracefulness. The otter's neck arched in the lilting movements that are uniquely its own. There were black strips on the ice where the snow had been scraped away as the otter slid on its belly on the ice, revealing an innate sense of playful fun.

River otters will play both in and out of the water, alone or in the company of others. We once watched a group of otters on a wooden boat dock, curling around each other to form a large roly-poly ball of wriggling brown fur. On another occasion, we counted seven otters slithering and cavorting over one another in the ocean, looking like one multi-tailed and multi-headed sea monster.

An otter seen in salt water is not necessarily a sea otter. River otters are common in many coastal areas and they often enter the ocean in search of food. The style of swimming is the key to identification — the sea otter swims on its back, propelling itself with its flipper-like back feet, while the river otter swims face down, with only its head and part of its back out of the water.

Sea otters are sea mammals in every sense — they eat, play, groom, and sleep in the ocean; they do go ashore at times, to escape violent storm conditions for example, but they never venture more than a few feet from the water, leaving few recognizable marks in their passage. The river otter, on the other hand, is primarily a land animal, and its tracks on land are not uncommon. The webs of the rear feet may leave distinctive marks in soft mud, damp sand, or snow. The track imprints are roundish, with five front and hind toes usually showing clearly. River otters normally leave groups of four tracks, thirteen to thirty inches apart, but can leap to eight feet and slide for great distances on their undersides.

River Otter
life size in mud

LYNX
Lynx canadensis

Order: Carnivora. Family: Felidae (cats). Range: widespread from British Columbia northward; central and eastern Washington and northeast Oregon. Habitat: woodlands and adjoining areas. Size and weight: three feet; thirty pounds. Diet: strictly carnivorous, chiefly snowshoe hare; some small mammals and birds. Sounds: quite vocal; hissing, spitting, growls, and caterwauling typical of cat family.

Closely related to the bobcat in size and characteristics, the lynx has adapted to its generally more northerly range with longer fur, conspicuous ear tufts, and larger paws that offer buoyancy in deep snow. The lynx relies on snowshoe hares as the mainstay of its diet. When the cyclic hares are abundant, the female lynx has larger litters, but when the hares are scarce, she may completely abstain from bearing offspring. The lynx hunts on the ground or in trees, and dens in rocky caves or hollow logs. It is a secretive, nocturnal animal that is rarely sighted in the wild.

Lynx and mountain lion ranges overlap in part and their feet are the same size, but the lynx trail is only about seven inches wide. Its walking stride is about twelve inches. The lynx is also much lighter and doesn't sink very deeply into snow or soft earth.

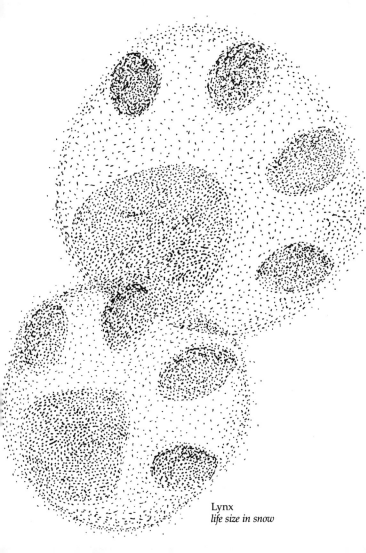

Lynx
life size in snow

MULE DEER
Blacktail deer

Odocoileus hemionus

Order: Artiodactyla (even-toed hoofed animals). Family: Cervidae (deer). Range: common throughout the Pacific Northwest including offshore islands. Habitat: forest and adjoining areas at all altitudes; regularly extending into cactus country. Size and weight: six feet; 200 pounds. Diet: strictly vegetarian, including leaves, grasses, grains, terminal shoots. Sounds: generally silent.

Our Pacific coast blacktail mule deer is somewhat smaller than the mule deer of the Rocky Mountain region, but it is now considered the same species. Active during the day and at dusk, it is fairly easy to spot in the wild and hard to confuse with any other animal. If you see black tail-markings and large mule-like ears, that's no elk, and there's no remotely similar animal in Pacific forests. These deer are usually solitary or gather in small groups. At first sign of a threat they flee in their distinctive, feet-together, bounding gait, with all four hooves landing and taking off at the same time. They are strong swimmers and like salt, so they can often be seen along ocean beaches, especially during the winter.

The mule deer's tracks are easy to identify: the small, slender hooves usually spread slightly at the heels and the dewclaws usually leave imprints. They leave tracks less than two feet apart when walking or in clusters every nine to twelve feet when bounding.

Mule Deer
life size in mud

MOUNTAIN GOAT   *Oreamnos americanus*

Order: Artiodactyla (even-toed hoofed animals). Family: Bovidae (cattle, sheep, and goats). Range: coastal southeastern Alaska and British Columbia through the Cascades of central Washington; also introduced into the Olympics. Habitat: mountainous regions, steep, high pastures, and rocky areas, usually just below snowline; often descend to sea level in winter. Size and weight: five feet; 250 pounds. Diet: strictly vegetarian, including grass, leaves, sedges, and lichen. Sounds: generally silent.

Mountain goats are stocky, heavily muscled animals with white fur coats and short black horns. Their hooves are superbly adapted for the mountainous terrain in which they live. A combination of hard outer edge and soft inner part affords them the animal-equivalent of rock-climbing shoes, and the only thing that can catch a healthy mountain goat in rocky areas is another goat. But even mountain goats hit loose holds now and then, and the resulting falls are often fatal. Consequently, these animals prefer to spend their time grazing high alpine pastures with a sentry or two posted, the herd returning to the rocks to escape wolves, biting flies, or wildlife photographers, none of which really bother them to any great extent.

Mountain goat tracks are fairly common near high alpine ponds and patches of dirt around the rocky areas they inhabit. Winter snows often force them down into deer country, but their tracks are always easy to identify because of the splayed hooves, lack of dewclaw imprints, and mode of running.

Mountain Goat
life size in mud

MOUNTAIN COTTONTAIL   *Sylvilagus nuttalli*

Order: Lagomorpha. Family: Leporidae (hares and rabbits). Range: central and eastern Washington and Oregon. Habitat: thickets, sagebrush, loose rocky areas; in wild country, into rural areas and outskirts of urban areas. Size and weight: thirteen inches; two to three pounds. Diet: green vegetation, as well as bark, twigs, and terminal shoots. Sounds: capable of a very loud squeal when extremely distressed, otherwise silent.

Cottontail rabbits are native to nearly all of the contiguous United States. They are active day and night, all year-around, and are generally plentiful due in part to the fact that each adult female produces three or four litters of four to seven young rabbits every year. Of course, they are high on the menu of a great variety of predators, also.

Pudgy little mountain cottontails, with their short ears, necks, and legs, make the snowshoe hare and especially the jackrabbit look quite gangly and awkward by comparison. That is, until the latter start running, and this is what makes recognition of rabbit and hare tracks fairly simple in the Pacific Northwest. The familiar rabbit track pattern seldom varies regardless of speed. But the squatty cottontail leaves track groups that span only six to nine inches, with only one to three feet between groups of prints when running. The whitetailed and blacktailed jackrabbits, which range over the same areas as the mountain cottontail, are quite long-legged animals that run powerfully and are capable of considerable speed. Consequently, their groups of four prints span from twelve to twenty-five inches, with groups of prints occurring from three to twelve feet apart, so they should never be confused with cottontail tracks. Finally, because jackrabbits run up on the toes of their hind feet, they often leave *smaller* hind foot imprints than either the snowshoe hare or mountain cottontail.

Other Pacific Northwest rabbits include the brush rabbit of western Oregon, which is very similar in appearance and track prints to the mountain cottontail, but generally does not overlap the cottontail's range; and the pygmy rabbit, which overlaps the cottontail's range in Oregon and southeastern Washington. This somewhat smaller version of the mountain cottontail will leave similar tracks, slightly smaller than, but easily confused with, those of an adult cottontail.

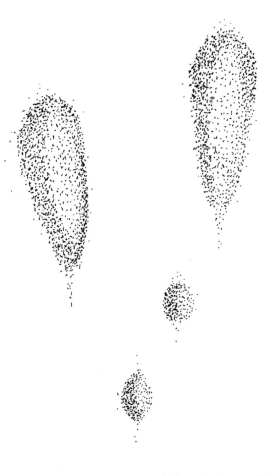

Mountain Cottontail
1/2 life size in snow

MOUNTAIN LION
Cougar, puma

Felis concolor

Order: Carnivora. Family: Felidae (cats). Range: a few wild isolated pockets in southern and central British Columbia, Washington, and Oregon. Habitat: swamps, thick forest, and mountainous regions below timberline. Size and weight: eight feet; 200 pounds. Diet: strictly carnivorous, mule deer, most other small mammals and birds, occasionally carrion. Sounds: screaming mating call and other cat noises with greater volume and timbre.

After being hunted to the verge of extinction, our large native American cat with its long, waving tail is now so scarce, nocturnal, and secretive in its ways that if it weren't for zoos, most of us would have no idea what it looks like. As you travel the Pacific Northwest, you at least have a chance to find evidence of the animal's presence. Since mountain lions have no natural enemies and raise two to five kittens every other year, the future could hold the promise for an increase in their numbers. The animals hunt on the ground and by dropping from trees, and they are an important natural control of the deer populations.

Mountain lion tracks are similar in size to those of the snowshoe-footed lynx, but may be distinguished by the angular shape of the pads. On soft surfaces the mountain lion sinks to a depth corresponding to its much greater weight. Also, spacing of tracks will be what you'd expect of the larger cat — trail width of twelve inches or more, walking tracks twenty-two inches apart, three feet separating pairs of trotting tracks, bounding leaps of twelve feet or more. Another sure sign is the tail drag marks that may be found, especially in snow. And of course, like all cats, mountain lions have retractile claws which never leave marks on any surface.

Mountain Lion
life size in mud

ELK
Wapiti

Cervus canadensis

Order: Artiodactyla (even-toed hoofed animals). Family: Cervidae (deer). Range: coastal forests of Vancouver Island, Washington and Oregon; also occasionally in central through eastern Washington. Habitat: prefer semi-open forested terrain. Size and weight: eight feet; 800 pounds. Diet: strictly vegetarian, including leaves and bark of trees including willow, pine, hemlock, aspen, and poplar; other succulent vegetation and grains. Sounds: various squeals, babbling and barking exhalations; also distinctive bugle call during autumn mating.

Second in size only to the moose among American deer, the elk is a herd animal whose numbers have been drastically reduced by hunters over the last century. The Pacific Northwest supports one of the few remaining isolated populations of elk on the continent. While cow elk do not have antlers, all elk can be identified by their yellowish-white rump patches and small white tails.

Within the Pacific Northwest, elk and moose ranges do not overlap, which makes signs left by elk easy to identify, from mud wallows to tooth marks on aspen or hemlock trees. Elk tracks are distinctively large, showing full rounded hooves. Their dewclaws often fail to leave imprints when the animal is walking, but on softer surfaces or when running, the elk's sheer weight drives its legs down, and the dewclaw imprints will be apparent.

Elk
life size in mud

WOLVERINE

Gulo luscus

Order: Carnivora. Family: Mustelidae (weasels). Range: rare throughout southeastern Alaska, British Columbia and south into the Cascades. Habitat: high-altitude forest and adjoining areas, alpine meadows and tundra, near and above timberline. Size and weight: 3½ feet; forty pounds; largest of North American weasels. Diet: strictly carnivorous, including all smaller animals and carrion. Sounds: normally silent; may snarl or growl when disturbed.

The wolverine looks and acts like a small brown bear with a long, fluffy tail, buffy stripes down its sides, and a very nasty disposition. This fierce, aggressive animal is extremely strong for its size, and even the largest predators will avoid a confrontation with a healthy adult wolverine. A wary, secretive animal inhabiting fairly remote and desolate places, it is infrequently sighted in the wild.

Once, on a mid-winter airplane flight, we spotted a wolverine on a high Alaskan lake. As we circled and landed on the windswept ice, the alarmed wolverine arched its back and danced sideways much like a cat might, leaving all manner of irregular-looking tracks, before disappearing into some nearby boulders. The tracks were the size of a wolf's, but even where the fifth toe didn't leave a print, the pad shape was still unique. The wolverine walks flat-footed, and if not all of its soles leave marks, at least the heel knob behind the main pad usually does. At the same spot we noted an interesting phenomenon in some older tracks: the wolverine's weight had compressed the snow beneath its feet, then the wind had blown away the soft, untracked snow around the imprint, leaving perfect tracks standing an inch above the lake ice.

Wolverine
½ life size in mud

GRAY WOLF
Timber wolf

Canis lupus

Order: Carnivora. Family: Canidae (dogs). Range: most common from British Columbia northward; rare from the Cascades through central Oregon. Habitat: forested and open areas from sea level to far above timberline. Size and weight: six feet; 150 pounds. Diet: generally carnivorous, including meat in any available form, from mouse to moose; some insects, vegetation, fruits, and berries. Sounds: barks, snarls, and growls; also long, mournful wail at night, not usually in chorus like coyotes.

A person who sights a gray wolf in the wild these days is fortunate indeed, for they have been systematically exterminated in most inhabited areas of the continent.

Gray wolves are intelligent, gregarious animals that mate for life and have quite complicated social organizations. They would seem to deserve protection from eradication. We have been quite close to these wolves on many occasions and can attest to the fact that they pose no threat to humans. The encounters have always been exciting and pleasurable.

Wolf tracks show the four toes and nails typical of all canines, with the front foot slightly larger than the rear. Angularity of pads and overall size distinguish wolf tracks, as no other canine leaves tracks five inches or more in length, nor covers ground like the gray wolf. Running wolves cover six to eight feet every four steps, with a walking stride of nearly two feet.

Gray Wolf
1/2 life size in mud

MOOSE

Alces alces

Order: Artiodactyla (even-toed hoofed animals). Family: Cervidae (deer). Range: common only in certain river valleys in southeastern Alaska; widespread through British Columbia, including Vancouver Island, extending south into northwestern Washington. Habitat: forests and adjoining areas, meadows, grasslands; often near rivers, lakes, and swampy bottomlands. Size and weight: six or more feet tall; 800 to 1100 pounds. Diet: vegetarian, including aquatic plants, leafy succulents, twigs, bark, terminal shoots. Sounds: generally silent, although both sexes capable of an astonishing range of whines, grunts, and other gutteral sounds, especially during the fall mating season.

Except for their great size and peculiar shape, we've found moose to be, in general, a fairly boring lot. Like all ruminant animals, they spend most of their waking hours slowly moving about and chewing. Their normal response to a perceived threat is to gallop wildly for a few hundred feet on legs marvelously adapted for running through high, thick brush, then to stop and resume their cud-chewing. Be that as it may, the bulls do put on quite a display in the autumn, jousting with massive racks of antlers; but beware, they can be quite unpredictably aggressive toward humans at that time of year, as can a cow with a young calf in the spring.

Differentiating deer family tracks can be tricky, but there is no problem with adult moose tracks. They are strikingly large, from five to seven inches in length and up to four feet apart even when walking. Juvenile tracks, however, can be confused with those of elk or mule deer where their ranges overlap. But remember that juvenile animals almost always travel with an adult, so you must search the immediate area for larger tracks. Habitat will be a clue, also. No other Pacific Northwest hoofed animal shares the moose's great affinity for water.

Finally, moose are not herd animals. A bull, cow, and two calves, is as large as a moose gathering gets, whereas mule deer and elk often congregate in larger numbers. Then again, four moose can make a lot of tracks by hanging around one small pond for an extended period of time. But the largeness of the adult track should provide positive identification.

Moose
1/2 life size in mud

SNOWSHOE HARE   *Lepus americanus*

Order: Lagomorpha. Family: Leporidae (hares and rabbits). Range: throughout the Pacific Northwest, except for major islands and parts of eastern Oregon. Habitat: forests, brushy areas, and swamps. Size and weight: eighteen inches; four pounds. Diet: grasses, willows, lupine, and other vegetation; buds of conifers, twigs, bark of alders, aspens, and willows. Sounds: thumps its feet; also screams, grunts, growls occasionally.

Most people should be familiar with the snowshoe hare — this medium-sized member of the rabbit family is active day and night, year-around, and is quite common over a large territory. It is aptly named since its unique hind feet have separable toes, allowing them to function like snowshoes when traveling on soft surfaces. In snowy areas the winter coat is white, changing predominantly to brown during the other seasons.

Although its range partially overlaps that of both the jackrabbit and cottontail, track recognition is easy, because of the natural snowshoe formed by its toes. A snowshoe hare's toes always spread out, leaving distinctively separate imprints. The length of each track pattern of four prints averages eleven inches; hopping length is about fourteen inches, while leaping distance is more than five feet.

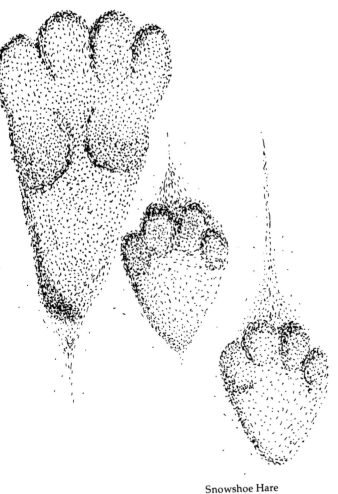

Snowshoe Hare
1/2 life size in snow

BEAVER

Castor canadensis

Order: Rodentia. Family: Castoridae (beavers). Range: throughout most of the Pacific Northwest including offshore islands. Habitat: near fresh-water streams and ponds in forested country and adjoining areas. Size and weight: 3½ feet; fifty pounds. Diet: strictly vegetarian, including aquatic plants, bark, twigs, and leaves of many deciduous trees. Sounds: non-vocal, but smacks tail on water when alarmed.

This industrious, aquatic mammal is the largest North American rodent. Although it sometimes lives unobtrusively on river banks, signs of the beaver's presence are quite obvious. It must provide itself with water for survival, which usually entails gnawing down dozens of small, soft-wood trees and constructing a conspicuous dam system, often several hundred yards long, and a lodge. Beavers can grasp objects with their front paws, and stand and walk upright on their rear feet. They use their flat, scaly, strong tails for support. Gregarious animals, beavers work well together on their engineering projects. They are active year-around, but may operate unobserved beneath the ice during much of the winter.

Beavers sometimes obscure portions of their tracks by dragging their tails over them. Still, the large webbed hind feet almost always leave distinctive imprints, with six to eight inches between pairs of tracks.

Beaver
1/2 life size in mud

BLACK BEAR
Cinnamon bear, glacier bear

Ursus americanus

Order: Carnivora. Family: Ursidae (bears). Range: widespread throughout the Pacific Northwest. Habitat: forests and adjoining areas at all elevations. Size and weight: seven feet; 450 pounds. Diet: omnivorous, including fish, small mammals, insects, fruits, berries, and succulent vegetation. Sounds: usually silent; grunts, whines, growls, clicks teeth, smacks jaw — all danger signals for smaller animals, including humans.

The black bear is the smallest and most common American bear. Smokey is a black bear, and we have grown accustomed to seeing these animals around rural garbage dumps and parks. In the wild, black bears are shy and wary of human contact and, consequently, harder to sight. They are good tree climbers, swim well, and can run twenty-five miles per hour for short stretches. They are very quick and strong. It could be dangerous to underestimate any black bear, and it could be downright unhealthy to get close to a mother bear with cubs.

Black bear tracks are usually impossible to mistake, being nearly human in both size and shape. The large claws leave prints wherever the toes do. Occasionally we have seen places where a bear has slipped on firm mud; its toes and claws did not register, but the smooth slide mark from the sole of the foot was distinctive. Be alert for small tracks, just the size of our drawing — you really don't want to get tangled up with those cubs!

Black Bear
½ life size in mud

BROWN BEAR   *Ursus arctos*

Order: Carnivora. Family: Ursidae (bears). Range: widespread through southeastern Alaska including many offshore islands, through British Columbia into northern Washington. Habitat: alpine meadows, prairies, and forested areas from sea level to above timberline. Size and weight: eight to eleven feet; 800 to 1600 pounds. Diet: omnivorous, including nearly any edible material, fish, small and some large mammals, birds, insects, fruits, berries, nuts, and succulent vegetation. Sounds: mostly silent, but may grunt, growl, chop jaws, and click teeth together when annoyed or alarmed.

If you are looking down at tracks over a foot long that look remotely like the ones illustrated, you've gotten yourself into brown bear country. Most people are beginning to agree that the hundred-odd variations on the "large brown hairy creature" theme are all the same animal. The brown bears of the Pacific coast tend to be larger and more reclusive, while those of the inland areas, commonly called grizzlies, are slightly smaller and generally more aggressive. But all brown bears have certain things in common: they are large beasts with prominent shoulder humps; they are very territorial; their behavior is unpredictable under the best circumstances; their eyesight is poor; they are faster and stronger than you'd expect; and they've killed animals larger than you.

In brown bear country, sane people walk slowly, talk and whistle, shake cans full of pebbles, and tie bells on their packs. Prolonged observations are best conducted from trees, as brown bears don't climb.

Brown Bear
1/4 life size in mud

BIRDS

DARK-EYED JUNCO

Junco hyemalis

Order: Passeriformes. Family: Fringillidae (buntings, finches, sparrows). Range: southeastern Alaska through Oregon. Habitat: northern fir and spruce forests, deciduous woodlands. Size and weight: length six inches, wingspan eight inches; 7/8 ounce. Diet: seeds, insects, berries. Sounds: chipping, trills.

Looking out your window at the winter landscape, you often see small flocks of gray, brown, and white juncos moving about in search of seeds on the surface of the snow. We frequently see networks of the juncos' lace-like tracks in the snow beneath our bird feeder. The juncos are attracted to the seeds that the chestnut-backed chickadees scatter in their quest for the coveted sunflower seeds in the wild bird mix. Juncos seem to like having an occasional sparrow travel with them during their winter forays.

The junco's tracks are typical of the vast number of smaller land birds that leave delicate lines on snow, sand, or mud of inland areas. The hind toe is about twice as long as the front toes. The tracks are found in groups of two because these birds hop instead of walk as they are feeding on the ground. The relative size of the tracks will give a clue to the identity of the maker, as will seasonal and other considerations, verified, of course, by actual sightings.

Dark-Eyed Junco
life size in snow

COMMON SNIPE   *Capella gallinago*

Order: Charadriiformes. Family: Scolopacidae (snipes and sand-pipers). Range: southeastern Alaska through Oregon. Habitat: wet meadows, bogs, and salt-water grassy marshes beyond the high tide line. Size and weight: length twelve inches, wingspan sixteen inches; four ounces. Diet: insects, aquatic larvae, snails, earthworms, small crustacea, seeds of marsh plants. Sounds: "zhak" and winnowing during summer display flight.

A snipe visited us frequently while we were housebuilding during the fall equinox storms when we most needed cheering up. It poked its long bill into the wet meadow mud nearby as it probed for a variety of foodstuffs. It seemed untroubled by our hammering, scurrying, and bad tempers as we tried to work as amateur carpenters in a monsoon.

During spring and summer at dusk or on overcast days, the snipe makes a tremolo sound with its feathers as it flies. On moonlit nights this "winnowing" sound is wonderfully eerie, sounding a bit like insane laughter.

The tracks of a snipe are scattered in damp, sandy areas. The front center toe is longer than the other two front toes. A small hind toe, typical of most shorebirds, is present, and the tracks are usually seen in a line.

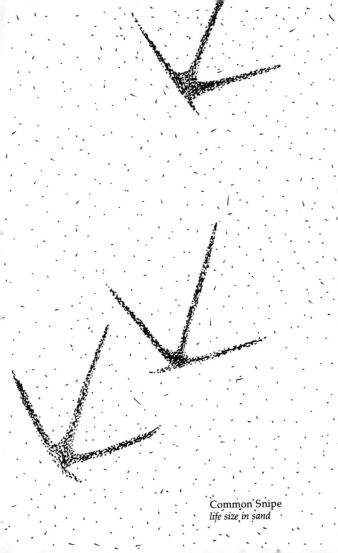

Common Snipe
life size in sand

NORTHWESTERN CROW   *Corvus caurinus*

Order: Passeriformes. Family: Corvidae (jays, magpies, crows). Range: southeastern Alaska through Oregon. Habitat: woodlands and open areas near tidewater shores. Size and weight: length sixteen inches, wingspan twenty-eight inches; fourteen ounces. Diet: eggs of other birds and small marine and aquatic organisms. Sounds: "khaaw, khaaw," "cowp, cowp, cowp," screams, cackles, coos, rattles, growls.

Crows are very vocal creatures. Research is beginning to uncover amazing aspects of their language and behavior such as the ability to count. Both wild and pet crows have been observed making up games to play. We once watched a northwestern crow flutter to the top of an eight-foot-long metal bannister, perch on it sideways, then slide down its entire length before hopping off.

Oftentimes observing crows helps you locate other wildlife. Groups of crows will mob and scold a predator such as an owl. They will perch near the animal, darting in to harrass and scold it.

At low tide the northwestern crow tracks should be fairly easy to find. All four toes in the track configuration are about the same length, each toe leaving a claw mark at the end. Crows walk and skip, so their tracks are not usually made in pairs.

Inland, the common crow is prevalent. Its tracks are identical in shape, perhaps slightly larger, and less common during non-snow seasons.

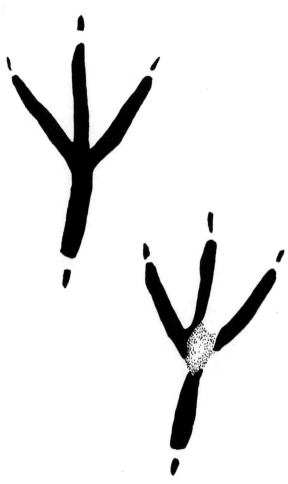

Northwestern Crow
life size in mud

GREAT HORNED OWL
Cat owl

Bubo virginianus

Order: Strigiformes. Family: Strigidae (owls). Range: southeastern Alaska through Oregon. Habitat: all habitats from forests to deserts with cliffs for nest sites. Size and weight: length twenty-three inches, wingspan fifty-two inches; 3½ pounds. Diet: rabbits, mice, rats, voles, skunks, grouse. Sounds: normally the male hoots four to five times while the female hoots six to eight times.

One spring day we spotted what looked like a cat sitting on a platform of sticks high up in a hemlock tree. It stared down at us with intense yellow eyes. This was a nesting "cat owl" more commonly called the great horned owl. The owl held the tufts of feathers on either side of its head in different positions which made it look remarkably like a cat. These owls nest so early in the spring that the brooding female is often partially covered with snow. They prefer to use nests constructed in previous years by hawks or ravens, rather than building their own.

When owls leave their nests, they fly through the forest without a sound. Special modifications of their wing feathers allow these night hunters to travel the airways in silence.

Owl tracks are uncommon, but owls do come down to the ground and pause long enough to leave a few tracks occasionally. They land to investigate and feed on food items that are too heavy to carry away or don't inspire them to do so. Car-killed animals are a good example and on recently rained-upon dirt roads, you may find owl tracks.

The tracks of the great horned owl in mud show the three thick and powerful talons it uses for grasping. The hind toe mark is just a small point.

Great Horned Owl
life size in mud

HERRING GULL   *Larus argentatus*

Order: Charadriiformes. Family: Laridae (gulls and terns). Range: southeastern Alaska through Oregon. Habitat: coastal areas, inland lakes and rivers. Size and weight: length two feet, wingspan four feet; 2½ pounds. Diet: fish, crustacea, marine worms, shellfish, sea urchins, insects, bird eggs. Sounds: "ke-ya-a-a, ke-ya-a-a," "hahaha," mews.

The herring gull is part of the poetry of the ocean as it glides overhead with its black-tipped wings. If it lands nearby, you will notice its yellow bill with a bright red dot on the lower half. This red spot figures prominently in the feeding of young gulls. When the chick pecks at this spot, it is fed by the parent.

Gulls nest on rocky islands. They vigorously defend their young with a variety of ruses. They will dive-bomb to attack a trespasser with their sharp bills, or they may disgorge food from their stomachs on the intruder.

The three front toes on the herring gull are connected by webs. It has a small hind toe that is elevated and does not make a track mark. In dry sand, clay, or mud the webbing may not leave an imprint. Viewing gull tracks in damp sand is the easiest way to see the molded imprints of its webbed feet.

Herring Gull
life size in sand

CANADA GOOSE

Branta canadensis

Order: Anseriformes. Family: Anatidae (ducks, geese, and swans). Range: southeastern Alaska through Oregon. Habitat: coastal mudflats, marshes, and lakes. Size and weight: length three feet, wingspan five feet; fourteen pounds. Diet: eel grass, grain, seeds, plant shoots; also roots, tubers, and leaves from aquatic plants. Sounds: "uh-whonk, uh-whonk," hisses when angry or alarmed.

Canada geese are commonly observed feeding in wet fields during early mornings and late afternoons, their black necks arching downwards to make strikingly curved patterns against the beige grass. When disturbed, they begin to call in unison, creating a wild cacophony of sound. Soon they take to the air, flying in V-shaped wedges.

Canadas mate for life. They nest on the ground near water, often choosing the small islets of beaver or muskrat houses as sites for their nests.

Typical of this family of birds, the Canada goose has four toes but the hind toe is elevated and does not leave an imprint. Its three main toes fan out in front and are connected by webs. The tracks are often seen on mud flats in conjunction with their squiggly sausage-shaped droppings.

Canada Goose
life size in mud

GREAT BLUE HERON   *Ardea herodias*

Order: Ciconiiformes. Family: Ardeidae (herons, egrets, and bitterns). Range: southeastern Alaska through Oregon. Habitat: fresh- and salt-water marshes, coastal mud flats, sand bars, shallow bays. Size and weight: length four feet, wingspan six feet; seven pounds. Diet: fish, snakes, insects, mice, and frogs. Sounds: "kraak," strident honks.

The presence of a great blue heron magically transforms a landscape, adding an aura of quiet beauty like that of a Japanese brush painting. The heron can be observed gracefully wading in shallow water as it seeks the fish that comprise a large part of its diet. A heron's nest, maintained year after year, is an elaborate structure of sticks three feet in diameter.

Great blue heron tracks are apt to be seen bordering the fresh- or salt-water areas where it feeds. It has four toes all on the same level. The hind toe is well-developed for standing and walking. A claw imprint shows clearly at the end of each toe.

Great Blue Heron
life size in mud

BALD EAGLE   *Haliaeetus leucocephalus*

Order: Falconiformes. Family: Accipitridae (hawks, kites, and eagles). Range: common through coastal Alaska and Canada; less common elsewhere, but slowly increasing. Habitat: coastlines of lakes, rivers, and oceans. Size and weight: length three feet, wingspan to seven feet; ten pounds. Diet: primarily fish; also carrion, small mammals, ducklings. Sounds: loud, abrupt, metallic "choik" or harsh "kleek-kik-ik-ik-ik."

These imposing, fairly shy birds are at once awesome and humorous. Where you find their tracks, you may spot them perched in evergreens or cottonwoods nearby, waiting for something edible to materialize, usually a fish. Their nests are likewise conspicuous — huge clusters of sticks resting atop old trees or cliffs. The first-hatched bald eagle is one of the only chicks of any eagle species that does not kill its later-arriving siblings; thus couples commonly raise two or three offspring each year. Immature bald eagles languish through four-year identity crises, during which their motley brown plumage is often mistaken for their less common golden cousins. The distinctive white head and tail feathers grow in the fifth year.

Eagles' talons are adapted for grasping, not walking, and they generally refrain from walking. You can expect to find only a few tracks in any one spot, usually around a fish carcass on a riverbank or ocean beach. Often only the toes leave prints, but the talon spread of up to six inches will readily identify the maker.

Bald Eagle
life size in mud

Recommended Reading

A Field Guide to Animal Tracks, by the eminent naturalist and wildlife artist Olaus J. Murie (1889-1963), is the classic work on the art of track identification. First published by Houghton Mifflin in 1954, it covers both common and rare mammals in North America, Mexico, and Central America. It also includes the tracks of some of the common birds, reptiles, amphibians and insects on our continent.

Snow Tracks by Jean George (E.P. Dutton), published in 1958, introduces the study of animal tracks to very young children.

Island Sojourn by Elizabeth Arthur (Harper and Row), published in 1980, is a painfully honest yet poetic account of what it's like to live on an island in British Columbia's wilderness for two years. The final chapter is a metaphysical discussion on the significance of animal tracks.

Index

Karen Pandell   Chris Stall

About the authors...

A love of wildlife and the outdoors drew Pandell and Stall from their native East Coast to a home base in Juneau, Alaska. From there they traveled the West Coast extensively for over ten years, from Prudhoe Bay to San Diego, observing, sketching and photographing wild animals in the field. They got even closer to their subjects during a year at Glacier Bay, Alaska, living in a cabin they built themselves (which lacked numerous amenities). Both Pandell and Stall are free-lance photographers, writers and artists, and have published articles in a number of outdoor and nature magazines. After collaborating on this book, the authors teamed up on a five-month, 6800-kilometer bicycle tour of Japan. Pandell now lives in New York, Stall in Alaska.

NOTES

NOTES

NOTES

NOTES

NOTES

NOTES